OCCASIONAL PAPER 4
written by Ian Smith

Building strong motivation

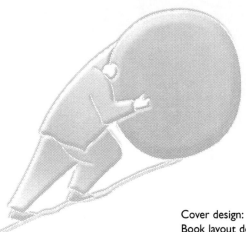

Cover design: Eva Ming Ling Kam
Book layout design: Susana Siew-Demunck

Originally published by Learning Unlimited
Republished in Australia by

HAWKER BROWNLOW
E D U C A T I O N

P.O. Box 580, Cheltenham,
Victoria 3192, Australia
Phone: (03) 9555 1344 Fax: (03) 9553 4538
Toll Free Ph: 1800 33 4603 Fax: 1800 15 0445
Website: http://www.hbe.com.au
Email: brown@hbe.com.au

© 2002 Learning Unlimited
© 2003 Hawker Brownlow Education

Code: #LUA-8894

National Library of Australia Cataloguing-in-Publication data:

Smith, Ian, 1947 Sep. 14–.
Building strong motivation.

For primary and secondary school teachers.
ISBN 1 74025 889 4.

1. Motivation (Psychology). 2. Child development.
I. Title. (Series: Smith, Ian, 1947 Sep. 14– Occasional
paper; 4).

370.154

Contents

Foreword

This is one of four occasional papers on the topic of motivation. The titles of the papers on this topic are:

Building strong motivation (Paper 4)

Can schools get beyond discipline? (Paper 5)

Positive thinking (Paper 6)

Self-esteem: not soft and not an option (Paper 7)

Building strong motivation sets the scene for the other three papers by looking generally at the issue of motivation – what it is and how it works. It examines some of the main ideas and beliefs underpinning the many theories about motivation, which have developed over the last hundred years. It focuses on what I have called 'strong' motivation and goes on to discuss if it is in fact the key life skill.

This paper is the fourth in a series of occasional papers. Each one draws on a wide body of research to summarise our current understanding about a key aspect of learning and teaching.

They are produced in the belief that it is critically important for teachers as professionals to reflect on the ideas and beliefs which underpin what they do in the classroom, and on the assumption that most teachers do not have the time or the energy to read lengthy academic texts at the end of a busy day in the classroom. They are short, and hopefully readable with further references given for those who want to explore further.

I am grateful to Robin Lloyd Jones and Bob Bissell for their support and help in putting this paper together, to Tony Bibby for graphics, to Liz Callaghan for proof reading, and to Joan Black, Centre for Education and Training Development, Glasgow Caledonian University for desk-top publishing and publication.

Ian Smith, January 2001

The top ten rules of motivation

Given your beliefs and experience of motivating yourself and helping other people to motivate themselves, how many of the following ring true to you?

1. Strong motivation comes from inside – it is about who you are, not just about what you want and it is closely related to the way you feel about yourself.

2. You can change the way you feel about yourself by changing the way you think and the way you act.

3. Ultimately you cannot motivate anyone else, but you can play a key role in helping other people to motivate themselves.

4. You can change the way you feel about yourself by changing the way you think and the way you act.

5. There is no one magic potion that will motivate everyone: we are each motivated in different ways.

6. Motivation, once established, doesn't last forever: you have to work at it on an ongoing basis.

7. If what you are doing at the moment (to motivate yourself or to motivate others) is not working, try something different.

8. Motivation is contagious: you must be motivated to motivate.

9. Motivation requires setting goals either by yourself or with others.

10. Competition and challenge will only motivate you if you are able to succeed: progress and success motivate – you get interested in what you are good at.

11. Team-working motivates; trust motivates; involvement motivates – where there is no involvement, there is no commitment.

'Strictly speaking the answer to the question "How do you motivate other people?" is "You can't!". The desire to do something, much less the desire to do it well, cannot be imposed. All we can do is maximise the chances of people developing an interest in what they are doing and remove the conditions that act as constraints on them.'

Douglas McGregor

Concerns about motivation in schools

> ❑   **motive:** a factor or circumstance that induces a person to act in a particular way.
>
> ❑   **motivate:** supply a motive to; be the motive of; cause (a person) to act in a particular way; stimulate the interest (of a person in an activity).

The Concise Oxford Dictionary

It seems that persuading young people to behave in what is considered an appropriate way and stimulating their interest in learning (in school at any rate) has always been a problem. In *Promoting Positive Discipline*, Pamela Munn traces the problem back to ancient Greece.

'Young people today love luxury. They have bad manners, they scoff at authority and lack respect for their elders. Children nowadays are real tyrants, they no longer stand up when their elders come into the room where they are sitting, they contradict their parents, chat together in the presence of adults, eat gluttonously and tyrannise their teachers.'

Socrates

She also refers to the synod of Aberdeen in 1675 which asked the presbyteries in Scotland to demand only three questions of the schoolmaster: whether he teaches them prayers for morning and evening, whether he says grace at meals and whether 'he chastises them for cursing, swearing, lying and speaking profanities, for disobedience to parents and what vices appear in them.'

Pamela Munn uses these examples to give her readers a sense of perspective. As she points out, it's very easy to form a distorted view of the problems of motivation in schools these days. The press regularly carry stories about the aggressive behaviour of pupils towards each other and their teachers.

'Every year it becomes harder and harder to cope, because there are fewer things you can do to control violent pupils and the government is simply trying to cover up the scale of the problem with youth in this country.'

Secondary teacher quoted in *The Scotsman*, May 2000

Certainly, a lot of evidence suggests that we should be concerned about the motivation of young people in schools today. But, despite the impressions the newspapers give, this evidence actually directs us not to the few pupils who are highly aggressive towards their peers or their teachers, but to the significant number who are disillusioned with school and who show their disillusionment in much less dramatic ways.

Michael Barber in *The Learning Game* discusses the findings of a 1994 survey of 30,000 pupils by Keele University on the attitudes of children in secondary schools in England. It is perhaps the most detailed work done in recent years into the attitudes of young people towards school.

The survey found that most young people were positive about school and said they worked as hard as they were able to. They thought that the school they attended was a good one and they generally felt welcomed there. But when the researchers probed a little further, they uncovered what Barber described as the 'disappeared', the 'disaffected' and the 'disappointed'.

The disappeared

☐   those who truant

☐   those who are excluded

☐   those who absent themselves through collusion ('don't bother me and I won't bother you').

'put together, these may add up to as many as 20% of 14–15-year-olds in secondary schools'

The disaffected

☐   almost 30% of pupils admit they behave badly sometimes or often

☐   a third of all pupils say that others in their class disrupt lessons every day

☐   almost half of all pupils say that others make fun of pupils who work hard.

The disappointed

☐   almost 60% agree that they 'count the minutes' to the end of their lessons

☐   over 20% believe that work is boring

☐   over 40% believe that lessons are too long.

Michael Barber concluded that 'a general lack of motivation affects perhaps 40% of all pupils in secondary schools.' This general lack of motivation has also been recognised by the Scottish Executive and they point to one of the reasons:

'An appreciable number of pupils do not find objectives which they see as relevant or attainable within the mainstream curriculum.'

Improving Achievements in Scottish Schools 1996 SOEID

This general lack of motivation and the low-level disruption it can cause in the classroom is a persistent problem for schools and an area in which many teachers want help.

The search for solutions

Given the concerns about motivation in schools, it is not surprising that the issue figures strongly in the workshops I run for teachers on learning and teaching. Many questions are raised about motivation, some of them frequently:

❑   How do you encourage children to do their best, not just the minimum?

❑   How do you get them to keep motivated?

❑   How do you motivate yourself in certain areas of the curriculum?

❑   How do you get fourth-year girls to bring their PE kit?

❑   How do you motivate the child to whom nothing seems to matter?

When we begin to search for the solutions to these very practical questions it often becomes evident that many teachers have become very pessimistic about their ability to motivate their pupils. A lot of teachers seem to believe, like the teacher quoted in the *Scotsman* article on page 6, that they have fewer and fewer ways to influence young people's motivation in school. Some of them have seen major changes in how schools have sought to motivate pupils over the years such as the change in emphasis from the use of punishments to the use of rewards. The new methods don't seem to them to work as well as they ought to – or as well as the old methods.

Also, when discussing motivation, many teachers seem to want to focus on factors which, although significant in terms of influencing pupils' motivation, are beyond their control. Rather than focusing on what they as teachers working in their own schools can do, they often want to discuss what parents should do, or what the government or society as a whole should do.

I have often used an idea developed by Stephen Covey in his book *The Seven Habits of Highly Effective People* to help teachers to be more aware of this problem and to focus on what they can actually do to motivate their pupils.

Stephen Covey suggests that the first and most important habit of people who are effective in any walk of life is that they are proactive – they take control over their own lives and no matter what happens to them, they focus on what they are able to do.

According to Covey, we have a circle of concern, inside of which are all of the things that we care about in life. We also all have a circle of influence – a smaller circle inside our circle of concern. In this circle are the things that we are concerned about and have the power to change.

Effective people, Stephen Covey suggests, do not spend too much of their time agonising about the things that are of concern to them but over which they have no influence. If they do that, they feel increasingly powerless. Those that work within their circle of influence, on the things that they are concerned about but also have influence over (no matter how small they believe that influence is) will achieve success, and their confidence and motivation will grow.

This can be a very powerful tool to help people build their confidence and motivation. It packs a particularly powerful message for teachers when linked to motivation. Teachers can identify lots of causes of pupil demotivation which, although genuine, are to a large extent outside their control. However, they are often reluctant to focus on the two areas where research consistently tells us that schools can make a difference, namely the ethos and climate in the school and the quality of learning and teaching in the classroom.

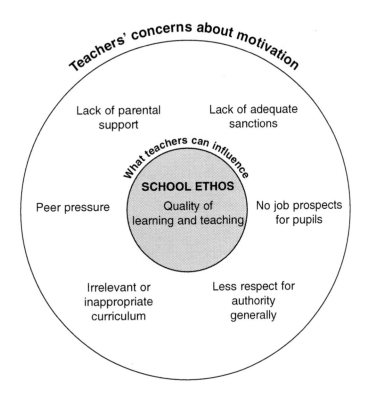

Examining the circles of concern and influence is actually a very practical way of helping teachers and schools to focus on what they can achieve in improving motivation without forgetting the other important factors which schools cannot deal with on their own.

There is no one best way

In workshops, teachers often express the desire for a magic potion or bullet either to motivate themselves or to help them motivate their pupils. These requests are usually light-hearted but they often spring from a serious desire to find a simple 'quick fix' or 'catch all' solution. Teachers often ask for instant advice and off-the-shelf prescriptions:

'Tell me how to motivate my class, I have tried everything!'

In fact, 'catch all' solutions and instant advice are widely available. That's part of the problem. There are too many of them. Motivation is becoming a major industry, not just an issue in school. Success in business depends on motivating yourself and others. Self-motivation is critically important in leading a happy and fulfilling life. Business gurus charge thousands of dollars for motivational talks and the shelves in the self-help sections of bookshops are groaning.

The key ideas in much of the motivation industry have been around for thousands of years. Over the last century in particular, motivation has been a central concern of psychology, producing a whole range of theories on the subject. Some can help us to examine our ideas about motivation and to understand why some techniques might be more useful than others.

But it is not a good idea to put your faith in any one theory. Most assume that people and situations are more alike than they actually are and to believe that one person, no matter how charismatic, can change your life for you in an afternoon is simply naïve, no matter how much many people seem to want to believe it.

It may be hard to accept, but the reality is that there is no one best way either to motivate yourself or to motivate other people.

❑   People are very different and very complicated.

❑   Motivation is a very personal thing; it depends on a whole range of factors such as personality, wants, needs, background, situation etc.

❑   What motivates us one day will not motivate us the next; our needs change and our moods swing back and forwards even more quickly.

❑   How we help others to motivate themselves depends greatly on our relationship with them.

#LUA-8894 © 2003 Hawker Browlow Education

Asking the deeper questions

If the bad news is that there is no one best way to build motivation, the good news is that there are lots of ways.

Over the past hundred years, psychology and neurology have given us a much better understanding about motivation and how it works. Many theories can help us to think more clearly about motivation and what it means to us. And many have been developed to provide practical techniques and approaches to motivation which can be used in different ways.

One thing is clear: because motivation is so individualised, finding out what will work best for us in our context means being able and willing to ask ourselves the deeper questions about motivation generally and about ourselves in particular. These deeper questions lie behind the practical questions posed by the teachers examined earlier. And in schools they are the questions we need to reflect on not only as individuals but together.

For instance:

What is motivation?

How does it work?

What motivates us?

How motivated are we?

As a growing number of people are coming to recognise, even this level of questioning is not deep enough. They point out that we have to go beyond the 'What?' and the 'How?' questions to the 'Why?' and the 'Who?' questions. Motivation for them is not just about psychology, but also about philosophy and morality. Questions about motivation are inextricably bound up with questions such as:

What do we believe in?

What are our values?

This paper gives a brief overview of some of the ideas underpinning our beliefs about motivation and our approaches to it. Its main purpose is to help teachers to reflect on these questions as a way of preparing themselves for the practical tasks of motivating themselves and of helping children to find ways of improving their own motivation.

Beliefs about human nature

One set of beliefs which directly affects our thinking about motivation is what being human means to us. We may not be consciously aware of them but we all hold a set of beliefs, mental models or assumptions about human nature.

Perhaps the best known way of describing these different assumptions was developed by a social psychologist, Douglas McGregor, in the 1960s. He described two sets of competing assumptions about human nature, which he called 'theory X' and 'theory Y'.

Theory X Assumptions about human nature	Theory Y Assumptions about human nature
❑ The average person has an inherent dislike of work and will avoid it if possible.	❑ The average person does not inherently dislike work. Depending on the onditions it may be a source of satisfaction or punishment.
❑ Because of this, most people must be coerced, controlled, directed or threatened with punishment, or bribed by rewards to get them to put in adequate effort.	❑ People will exercise self-direction and self-control in the pursuit of objectives to which they are committed.
❑ The average person prefers to be directed, wishes to avoid responsibility, has relatively little ambition and wants security above all.	❑ The average person learns under proper conditions, not only to accept, but to seek responsibility. Many more people are able to contribute to the solutions of organisational problems than do so.

The pessimistic (or cynical?) view:

'We are frightened by the idea that there is such a thing as original sin and that men have a natural capacity for evil.'

Digby Anderson and Peter Mullen, *Faking It*

#LUA-8894 © 2003 Hawker Browlow Education

McGregor's theory has been popular on business courses but I find that not many teachers have come across it. Nevertheless, it can be used it to stimulate discussion through the following activity:

Map where you think you and then your school fall between theory X and theory Y below.

Share and compare your responses and discuss the reasoning behind them.

You

X .... **Y**

Your school

X .... **Y**

Only a few teachers will admit to subscribing entirely to theory X or to theory Y. Theory Y is seen as being naïve: theory X is cynical. Most put themselves somewhere between the two or suggest that they subscribe to both. They will say 'it depends' – depends on the way they are feeling on a particular day, on the context within which they are trying to motivate etc.

It usually leads to a good discussion about motivation and allows different perspectives to be discussed, for instance between primary and secondary teachers. It certainly helps people to recognise that they have beliefs about human nature and that these views inevitably affect not only their views about motivation but their practice in the classroom.

The optimistic (or sentimental?) view:

'*The innermost core of man's nature, the deepest layers of his personality, the base of his 'animal nature' is basically positive.*'

Carl Rogers, *On Becoming a Person*

The balanced (or realistic?) view:

'*Unfortunately, man is on the whole, less good than he imagines himself or wants to be.*'

Carl Jung

Theories about motivation

McGregor's theories about human nature reflect one of the key debates about motivation which have occupied psychologists for the past eighty years – the nature and relative importance of intrinsic and extrinsic motivation. These can be defined as follows:

Extrinsic motivation	Intrinsic motivation
Is when you are motivated to do something not because you enjoy it for its own sake or because you feel it is worthwhile, but because you feel obliged or compelled to do it or because it will help you to achieve a goal which someone else thinks is important for you.	Is when you are motivated to do something because you really want to do it for its own sake or because it will help you attain a goal which you have freely chosen because it is important and worthwhile to you personally.

This suggests that there are two ways of motivating others: from the outside by the threat of punishments or the promise of rewards or from the inside by using people's positive states to draw them into a task of their own volition.

If you subscribe to McGregor's theory X, you are likely to support an outside-in approach. If you prefer theory Y, you are likely to support an inside-out approach.

Over the past fifty years debates about extrinsic and intrinsic motivation have been taken to extremes. Those who support extrinsic motivation seem to believe that people are naturally selfish and lazy, that they see work as unpleasant and learning as difficult, a chore. They work, therefore, not because they enjoy it, but to earn money to do the things they want to do when they are not working. They claim that:

There is no such thing as intrinsic motivation

- ❑   learning is generally a difficult and unpleasant thing and, given the chance, we will avoid it

- ❑   people are primarily driven by extrinsic factors such as money, promotion or fear

- ❑   the teacher's role is to make people learn

#LUA-8894 © 2003 Hawker Browlow Education

This extreme view is well expressed in the views of the philospher, Bantock, who claims,

'Interest is largely the creation of circumstance. It is not something a child is born with and it is up to the teacher to create.'

The opposite point of view can be traced in modern times to Rousseau but has its roots in the ancient world. It has strongly influenced the child-centred schools of thought on learning and teaching which were popular in the 1960s and 1970s in the UK and the USA.

This view stresses the paramount importance of intrinsic motivation. It is a survival skill. We are born with an innate desire for learning and an unlimited confidence in our own ability to learn and this confidence is well founded. We are remarkably able learners. The key assumptions of this view strongly expressed are:

Nothing matters but intrinsic motivation

- ❑ learning is generally a natural and enjoyable activity. We do it all the time, in fact we can't not do it

- ❑ people are driven primarily by intrinsic factors such as the love of learning and a natural curiosity

- ❑ the teacher's role is to get out of the way and let people learn

Taking extreme positions on the concepts of intrinsic and extrinsic motivation does not make sense. Given the position he takes, it is difficult to believe that Bantock has ever been around young children, but it is also difficult to imagine how a teacher could function effectively while advocating the extreme opposite view. Motivating young people is a fundamental part of what it is to be a teacher.

Indeed the words 'intrinsic' and 'extrinsic' can be confusing. Psychologists have talked as if they are completely different from each other, but in reality it is not always possible to separate the two and most of us are motivated by a mixture of both. Sometimes an activity is undertaken both for the satisfaction it brings and as a means to an end. For instance, many people do a job because they enjoy it as well as for the salary. Pupils can study history not for the love of the subject, but because they want to get grades or because they want to please the teacher; all of these reasons can be considered intrinsic.

Nevertheless, the concepts of extrinsic and intrinsic motivation can help us to understand different approaches to motivation and our own attitudes to them.

Different approaches to motivation

Motivation is so complex it is hard to find a way through it. What follows next provides a kind of map by describing three broad approaches. Although they are different, they are related and all of them are used in schools to a greater or lesser degree. In fact, good teachers tend to juggle all three.

First, there are the 'positive discipline' approaches, which are much in vogue in schools. They are essentially 'outside-in' approaches. They focus on behaviour and look at changing and controlling other people's behaviour using a mixture of rewards and punishments. They are dealt with in more depth on page 17 of this paper and Occasional Paper 5, *Can schools get beyond discipline?*, provides an extended discussion.

Second, there are the 'positive thinking' approaches, which have been around for some time. They come mainly from the United States and are essentially 'inside-out' approaches. They focus on thinking and seek to change the way you feel by changing the way you think. We look at them in more depth on pages 18–19 of this paper and Occasional Paper 6, *Positive thinking*, is devoted to them.

Third there is what can be called the 'self-esteem movement'. It also places a very strong emphasis on 'inside-out'. The focus is on the self: self-awareness, self-acceptance, self-worth. The emphasis here is on feelings but the focus is very much on the whole person, with a recognition that motivation is about how we think and how we act as well as how we feel. We look at these approaches in more depth on pages 20–21 of this paper and Occasional Paper 7, *Self-esteem: not soft and not an option*, is devoted to them.

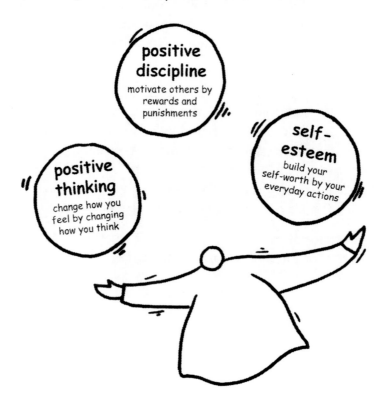

Outside-in approaches: positive discipline

'Reward it is that makes us good or bad'

Herrick quoted in Kevin Weldall and Frank Merrett,
Positive Teaching: The Behaviourist Approach

Positive discipline approaches are based on behaviourist theories of motivation. To motivate other people, they say, we should focus on their behaviour, not the causes of their behaviour (the thoughts and feelings that go on in their heads). You can see and influence behaviour, even control it; you cannot see, let alone control, what goes on inside a person's head. People can change their behaviour and you can influence them to do so by the judicious use of rewards and punishments or what are called euphemistically positive and negative reinforcers:

	To increase behaviour	To decrease behaviour
Deliver	**'good things'** praise gold stars sweets rewards	**'bad things'** reprimands punishment
Remove	**'bad things'** escape from nagging threats	**'good things'** losing privileges money opportunities

Behaviourist approaches are attractive to teachers and schools because they are easy to use and seem to offer simple solutions. If someone is misbehaving in the classroom, you need quick answers.

Evidence does suggests that, in the short term, positive discipline systems can be very effective in helping to create order in schools. But a significant body of research also suggests that there are a number of major problems with rewards, particularly where too much emphasis is placed on them.

Rewards can further demotivate those who do not get them and, if this problem is overcome by producing rewards for all, the value attached to the rewards is then reduced. Reliance on rewards can also be created, which means that motivation cannot be sustained without them. A more serious yet subtle finding is that strong extrinsic reward systems tend to undermine the motivation of those who get them. If an activity is of intrinsic interest in itself and is rewarded in an extrinsic way, children's intrinsic interest tends to wane.

Hence the need for schools to look beyond reward systems to approaches that focus on what goes on inside young people's heads, on their thoughts and feelings.

Inside-out approaches: positive thinking

'The ancestor of every action is a thought'

Ralph Waldo Emerson

'Positive thinking' has its roots in cognitive psychology and cognitive therapy and grew up in the United States in the 1970s. In the last decade it has become increasingly popular on both sides of the Atlantic, especially in the corporate sector and in sport. It is the basis of a set of personal development techniques known as neuro-linguistic programming (NLP) and is offered by a growing number of motivational 'gurus' such as Anthony Robbins in the USA and Jack Black in the UK.

The focus is on working on your goals to achieve success. There is a strong emphasis on self-belief, and the idea that we are mainly determined by our past is rejected. Also, we do what we do because we have the ability to contemplate the future – to hope. We have the power of conscious choice over what we achieve and what kind of person we become, and we all have a freedom and a responsibility to use that power.

The basic premise is that we can change the way we feel and act by changing the way we think. Optimism and hope – just like helplessness and despair – can be learned. We can help others to motivate themselves by helping them to be aware of and to change the way they habitually think about themselves and about events in their lives.

The proponents of positive thinking emphasise its practicality. They claim it provides a series of step-by-step procedures towards excellence. Indeed, many practical techniques are associated with positive thinking. Several involve finding better ways to communicate with yourself, tapping into the power of the subconscious mind and making more use of the abilities associated with the right side of the brain (see Occasional Paper 1, *How the brain learns*) including relaxation, focusing attention, visualisation, self-talk and affirmations.

18

The crucial role of self-belief in motivation and success is well documented in the many studies that have been made of successful people in many fields. Henry Ford's assertion, 'If you think you can, you can. If you think you can't, you can't' is typical of the view expressed in the business world. At the top levels of sport, the importance of mental as well as physical training is now well recognised.

We all use some aspects of positive thinking in our lives, but most of us do so without being aware of it. We don't use the techniques systematically and we have never been taught to do so. On the whole, these techniques are still not taught in schools today, despite the potential they have for raising achievement in examinations and for helping children develop some key life skills. Why is that?

There are cultural reasons. For many people, the idea of positive thinking is associated with the American 'go for it', 'have a nice day' mentality. It seems to fit uneasily into our culture, where we tend to be more sceptical and less inclined to talk positively about ourselves or to celebrate our achievements too openly.

In the Western world in general, we are distrustful of the idea of tapping into our subconscious mind and sceptical about the value of doing so. The idea of closing your eyes or admitting to the fact that you have an inner voice in public is scary stuff. Most teachers have not used these techniques consciously themselves and are unwilling to use them with young people. There is also the fear that, if they did, they would be accused of manipulation or brain washing.

There is also a question of values. Although people who practise positive thinking have a range of personal values, it has come to be associated in many people's minds with material aspirations. Success is seen as earning a lot of money or having a lot of possessions. Excellence is usually about winning. The title of one of the definitive books, Napoleon Hill's *Think and Grow Rich*, illustrates this. The gurus promise that by taking their advice you can double or triple your income in 90 days. Although they usually promise emotional, spiritual and physical fulfilment into the bargain, the emphasis is very much on outward success rather than inner fulfilment.

It does not help when the 'gurus' appear to promise instant, automatic and dramatic success ('your life will never be the same again', 'it only works') and underplay the need to work at the techniques. As a result, it is easy to see the techniques as being simplistic and gimmicky. Many people, for instance, find advice like 'smile at yourself in the mirror for 30 seconds every morning' impossible to take seriously, even if it might actually do them good to practise it.

Inside-out approaches: self-esteem

'Of all the judgements we pass in life, none is more important than the judgement we pass on ourselves.'

Nathaniel Branden, *The Six Pillars of Self Esteem*

Another set of inside-out approaches which have significant differences from positive thinking but with areas of overlap, focus on the importance of self-esteem. These are values-based psychological systems which stress beliefs, emotions and feelings together with the importance of relationships and what is called 'self-actualisation' or 'self-realisation'. The focus is on working on yourself to achieve personal happiness and fulfilment.

The basic premise is that people are important, your life is important. 'Being all you can be' is the noblest goal of your existence. Achievement itself is not all: the key is to develop the capacity to achieve and the development of a sense of your own self-worth is critical in this. Self-esteem is not to be found in possessions, status or power. These can offer us comfort but self-esteem is an intimate experience that lies within the core of our being. It does not come through measuring yourself against other people or being superior to them. What I think and feel about myself is crucial, not what anyone else thinks and feels about me. The tragedy is that people look for self-esteem everywhere but inside themselves.

Abraham Maslow is considered by many to be the father of these humanistic approaches to psychology. Since he first stressed the fundamental importance of higher-order needs in motivation, a huge amount has been written about self-esteem.

A hierarchy of needs

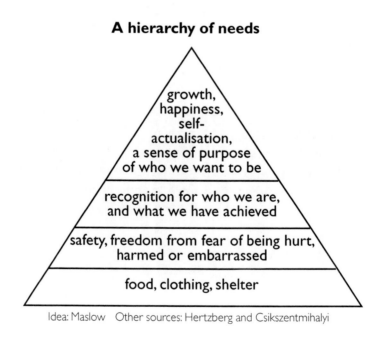

growth, happiness, self-actualisation, a sense of purpose of who we want to be

recognition for who we are, and what we have achieved

safety, freedom from fear of being hurt, harmed or embarrassed

food, clothing, shelter

Idea: Maslow   Other sources: Hertzberg and Csikszentmihalyi

The success of *Emotional Intelligence* by Daniel Goleman has helped raise awareness of the importance of the emotions in learning and in life. Goleman defines emotional intelligence as being aware of and in control of your own feelings and having empathy for the feelings of others. He draws strongly on recent research on the brain to confirm the critical role that emotions play in our lives. Such research has shown that thinking and feeling are inseparable from each other, and that, in our heads, feelings play a stronger role than thinking (see Occasional Paper 1). Goleman calls motivating yourself 'the master emotion' and claims it can be learned.

While positive thinking has been slow to catch on in education, self-esteem has struck a chord. There is a strong self-esteem movement in education in both the US and the UK. It has been particularly vigorous in the primary and early-years sectors where it fits well with the philosophy of educating the whole child.

A range of personal and social development programs have been devised around the concept of self-esteem and techniques such as circle time have grown up to promote and develop self-esteem.

But, as Nathaniel Branden, one of the most respected writers on self-esteem over the past thirty years, admits in his book *The Seven Pillars of Self Esteem*, many people have claimed too much for self-esteem. They seem to suggest, he says, that a healthy sense of self-value is all we need to assure happiness and success and this is patently not true. Self-esteem is not an all-purpose panacea. Although it may increase the likelihood that we will acquire the knowledge and skills we need to operate effectively in the world, it is not a substitute for them.

He also points out that self-esteem has been misused in schools and has led to self-delusion and wishful thinking, where children have been praised for virtually anything, consequently neglecting the importance of real accomplishments.

Those who view the whole idea of building self-esteem with suspicion have made capital as a result. In a recent book, *Faking It: The Sentimentalisation of Modern Society*, Bruce Cooper and Dennis O'Keefe claim that education has 'put aside discipline and obedience and replaced them with false standards'. They describe self-esteem as 'a myth' and 'a nonsense' and claim that it has led to a softening of standards and a lack of rigour and challenge in schools. Melanie Philips in her book, *All Must Have Prizes*, makes similar charges.

For these reasons it is important to argue a strong case for the benefits of building self-esteem and to ensure that schools go about it in an appropriate way. Occasional Paper 7 *Self-esteem: not soft and not an option* is devoted to looking at these issues in depth.

What is 'strong' motivation?

All of the approaches described on pages 17–21 can help people to be motivated and to motivate other people. Each approach is examined in greater detail in the next three occasional papers in this series. But to what extent do these approaches help to build 'strong' motivation? Before we can explore this question it is important to define 'strong' motivation and to discuss why it is so important.

First, motivation is usually attached to something. It makes sense to describe someone as a confident person, an optimistic person, even a happy person. But to describe someone as a motivated person begs a whole lot of questions: motivated to do what? to be what? to have what?

Second, although motivation is linked to happiness (if you are not motivated to do anything in life you are unlikely to lead a happy or successful life) it is by no means a good thing per se. You can be motivated to do things which most people would agree are extremely 'bad'. Driving your car at 200 km/h on the open road, for example, may give you a buzz, but it's probably not a good thing either for you or for anyone else using the same road.

Finally, it doesn't follow that the more motivated you are the better, even if what you are motivated to do is generally regarded as a 'good thing'. People who are too motivated become obsessive, addicted, fanatical; in effect, sad people in every sense of the term.

These moral and philosophical considerations aside, the following offers a definition of 'strong' motivation:

Strong motivation might be described as motivation which lasts:

❑   over a period of time

❑   through difficult times

❑   when the payback seems a while away

❑   when no-one is around to encourage you or force you to carry on.

'He who has a why can bear almost any how.'

Nietzsche

If you accept this definition, it is worth considering what people who have a capacity for such motivation (yet avoid becoming obsessive) are like. What attributes do they have? How do they behave? Here are some suggestions:

Those with strong motivation:	Those with weak motivation:
make an effort	don't make an effort
concentrate	are easily distracted
persevere	lack reliance and give up easily
are self-reliant	are dependent on others
can work independently	need constant supervision
take the initiative	want to be told what to do
are willing to tackle complex problems	look for simple answers
can deal with uncertainty	fear change
are prepared to make mistakes	fear failure
recognise the value of criticism	avoid criticism
know what they want	don't know what they want
feel good about themselves	have a poor self-image
are optimistic	feel helpless

However, these attributes are not just the effects of strong motivation: they cause it, and indeed may be prerequisites for it. If we do not have strong self-belief and strong self-esteem, our capacity for strong motivation will be significantly diminished.

Strong motivation is important in life

If you agree that the characteristics listed on pages 22–23 are an accurate reflection of someone with a capacity for strong motivation then it is not hard to see why building 'strong' motivation is so important, not just in school, but in life.

The Economy

More and more we are told that businesses who want to survive in a rapidly changing and increasingly competitive global economy cannot afford to be hierarchical, assuming that employees can only do what they are told and need someone standing over them to ensure that they do it.

Daniel Goleman (*Emotional Intelligence*) points to the growing amount of evidence which suggests that, to be successful in any walk of life, including a career, emotional intelligence is more important than academic intelligence. (see Occasional Paper 2, *Changing our minds about intelligence*).

Peter Senge in *The Fifth Discipline*, his seminal book on learning organisations, also suggests that modern organisations need to create the conditions which can tap people's potential to the full.

'We need to rethink our traditional views of motivation. This means setting aside the assumption that people are primarily motivated by rewards, punishments, or getting good grades and instead assuming that, in the right atmosphere, young people will contribute and make commitments because they want to learn, to do good work for its own sake and be recognised as people.'

Peter Senge

Society

As we grow richer as a society, we seem to become unhappier. This is the main message of *Britain on the Couch*, by clinical psychologist, Oliver James. He claims we are now unhappier despite being richer and quotes scientific evidence charting the rise in rates of depression since 1950. He goes on to explore why this is the case, and points out that modern life makes us feel losers even when we are winners. He suggests that therapy or medication will not solve the problem, only fundamental changes in the way we are organised as a society.

According to James, schools are a key part of the problem. Schooling, he says, has become increasingly competitive and points to the many academic studies which have demonstrated the damage that this can do to self-esteem. He quotes Diane Ruble, an education researcher who has found that schoolchildren who feel they may be failing (even although they are doing well) have no escape from the comparative system and often react by becoming less engaged or dropping out. James even describes his own former school as 'a system for undermining self-esteem'.

Is self–motivation the core skill?

To where does this quick tour through the complex topic of motivation lead? I believe it points clearly to the fundamental importance of helping children to develop and build their capacity for self-motivation, and the critical role of self-belief and self-esteem in building that capacity.

The qualities of a strongly motivated person outlined on page 23 are not those which someone else can just give to you. Although other people can create the conditions within which you can develop them, and help you to do so, ultimately they come from the inside out.

Building self-motivation should be an end in itself, not simply a means of helping children do well in school. Indeed, the school system should be charged with sending children out at the end of their education as eager to learn and as confident in their ability to do so as they came in.

Having stressed the importance of self-motivation, however, there are two caveats. First, schools will always have to use outside-in methods to motivate children: they will not, in their present form at any rate, be able to scrap their discipline systems. The real challenge lies in how to use extrinsic motivation without undermining intrinsic motivation and this is explored in the next occasional paper in the series.

Second, if there is a case for arguing that self-motivation is the core skill, it is certainly not the only one, nor can it be separated from other important skills. Being strongly motivated to learn is not enough. Children need to have the opportunity to learn and be able to do so. In fact, motivation and achievement are closely interlinked. Motivation can lead to achievement. And, as a number of eminent educationists have pointed out, it can also work the other way round.

'Being able to do comes very close to wanting to do. The best motivation is achievement.'

Michael Marland

'We get interested in what we are good at.'

Jerome Bruner

Young people will only develop strong motivation if they learn how to learn and become successful learners. To do so they need to be challenged as well as supported.

The implications for schools

There are profound implications for teachers, schools and the education system as a whole if we accept the messages of the theories and approaches discussed in this paper. The implications go well beyond learning and teaching in the classroom to personal and professional development for teachers and how we run our schools. They include:

❑ **recognising that schools and teachers make a difference**

Acknowledging that schools and teachers can and do create interest and motivation and build young people's self-belief and self-esteem.

❑ **rethinking our traditional models of motivation**

Playing down the role of rewards, competition and comparing young people with each other, and playing up the role of progress against individual goals and targets through personal development plans.

❑ **viewing personal and social development as the central and most important subject in the curriculum**

Recognising the importance of educating the whole child in secondary school as well as in primary school and viewing the building of strong motivation as an end in itself in school and not simply as a means to an end.

❑ **teaching young people a range of skills and techniques to help them motivate themselves**

Teaching optimism rather than helplessness, involving techniques like goal setting, assertiveness and positive thinking.

❑ **tackling teachers' own motivation and morale**

Appreciating that teaching is essentially an emotional activity and creating the conditions where teachers can develop personally and professionally without the perceived costs of doing so exceeding the likely benefits.

❑ **developing schools as learning organisations**

Ensuring that they are emotionally positive and supportive workplaces, where hierarchy is played down and team-working is encouraged.

❑ **ensuring that teaching is no longer an isolated activity.**

Helping teachers to work together in the classroom to support and learn from each other and to experience at first hand how they relate to children individually and collectively.

#LUA-8894 © 2003 Hawker Browlow Education

References and further reading

27 Ways to Improve Classroom Instruction Gary Phillips and Maurice Gibbons, Hawker Brownlow Education, Melbourne, 1996

All Must Have Prizes Melanie Phillips, Warner, London, 1998

Awaken the Giant Within Tony Robbins, Fireside, New York, 1991

Becoming an Achiever: A Student Guide Carolyn Coil, Hawker Brownlow Education, Melbourne, 1994

Britain on the Couch Oliver James, Arrow Books, London, 1998

The Craft of the Classroom: A Survival Guide Michael Marland, Heinemann, London, 1975

The Culture of Education Jerome Bruner, Harvard University Press, 1996

Emotional Intelligence Daniel Goleman, Bloomsbury, London, 1996

Faking It Digby Anderson and Peter Mullen (eds), Penguin Books, London, 1998

The Fifth Discipline Peter Senge, Random House, London, 1992

Freedom and Authority in Education Bantock, Faber and Faber, London, 1952

The Human Side of Experience Douglas McGregor, McGraw Hill, New York, 1960

The Learning Game Michael Barber, Victor Gollancz, London, 1996

The Motivation Pocket Book Max Eggert, Management Pocketbooks Ltd, Hants, 1999

Motivation and Personality Abraham Maslow, Harper, New York, 1954

Positive Teaching: The Behaviourist Approach Kevin Wheldall and Frank Merrett, Unwin Education, 1984.

The Principles of NLP Joseph O'Connor and Ian McDermott, Thorsons, London 1996

Promoting Positive Discipline Scottish Office, Moray House Publications, Edinburgh 1999

Raising Achievement: Strategies for Success Carolyn Coil, Hawker Brownlow Education, Melbourne, 2000

The Seven Habits of Highly Effective People Stephen Covey, Simon and Schuster, London, 1989

The Six Pillars of Self Esteem Nathaniel Branden, Bantam Books, 1995

Social Skills: Empowering Kids Sue Berne, Hawker Brownlow Education, Melbourne, 2001

Student Motivation: A Collection of Articles Hawker Brownlow Education, Melbourne, 2000

'There are Fewer Things You Can Do to Control Your Pupils' Stuart Nicolson, *The Scotsman*, 11 May, 2000

Think and Grow Rich Napoleon Hill, Hawthorn Books, New York

Unlimited Power Tony Robbins, Fireside, New York, 1997

Notes